THE FIRST BOOK OF BARITONE/BASS SOLOS

compiled by Joan Frey Boytim

ISBN 978-0-7935-0367-4

G. SCHIRMER, Inc.

DISTRIBUTED BY

HAL•LEONARD®
CORPORATION

7777 W. BLUEMOUND RD. P.O. BOX 13819 MILWAUKEE, WI 53213

PREFACE

Repertoire for the beginning voice student, whether teenager, college student, or adult, always poses a great challenge for the voice teacher because of the varied abilities and backgrounds the students bring to the studio. This series of books for soprano, mezzo-soprano and alto, tenor, and baritone and bass provides a comprehensive collection of songs suitable for first and second year students of any age, but is compiled with the needs of the young singer in mind.

In general, students' first experiences with songs are crucial to their further development and continued interest. Young people like to sing melodious songs with texts they can easily understand and with accompaniments that support the melodic line. As the student gains more confidence, the melodies, the texts, and the accompaniments can be more challenging. I have found that beginning students have more success with songs that are short. This enables them to overcome the problems of musical accuracy, diction, tone quality, proper technique, and interpretation without being overwhelmed by the length of the song.

Each book in this series includes English and American songs, spirituals, sacred songs, and an introduction to songs in Italian, German, French and Spanish. Many students study Spanish in the schools today, and most studio volumes do not include songs in this language; therefore, we have included two for each voice type.

Several songs in the collections have been out of print in recent years, while others have been previously available only in sheet form. Special care has been taken to avoid duplication of a great deal of general material that appears in other frequently used collections. These new volumes, with over thirty songs in each book, are intended to be another viable choice of vocal repertoire at a very affordable price for the teacher and student.

Each book contains several very easy beginning songs, with the majority of the material rated easy to moderately difficult. A few songs are quite challenging musically, but not strenuous vocally, to appeal to the student who progresses very rapidly and who comes to the studio with a great deal of musical background.

In general, the songs are short to medium in length. The ranges are very moderate, yet will extend occasionally to the top and the bottom of the typical voice. The majority of the accompaniments are not difficult, and are in keys that should not pose major problems. The variety of texts represented offers many choices for different levels of individual student interest and maturity.

In closing, I wish to thank Richard Walters at Hal Leonard Publishing for allowing me to be part of this effort to create this new series of vocal collections. We hope that these books will fill a need for teachers and students with suitable, attractive and exciting music.

Joan Frey Boytim

CONTENTS

ACROSS THE WESTERN OCEAN

sea chanty
arranged by Celius Dougherty

We are going a - way from friends and home, Oh, sai - lor, where you bound to? We're going a - way to search for gold, A - cross the west - ern o - cean.

Fa - thers, moth - ers,— say good - bye, Oh, sai - lor, where you—

bound to? Sis-ters, broth - ers, don't you cry, O'er the west - ern

o - cean. Oh, the

THE BLIND PLOUGHMAN

Marguerite Radclyffe-Hall

Robert Coningsby Clarke

Moderate time

with force

Set my hands up - on the plough, My feet up - on the sod:

Turn my face to - wards the east, And praise be to God!

THE BELLS OF CLERMONT TOWN

Blaire Belloc

A. M. Goodhart

13

BLOW, BLOW, THOU WINTER WIND

William Shakespeare

Roger Quilter

Tempo I.

Tempo I.

vigoroso.

mf

Freeze, freeze, thou bit - ter sky, That

mf

dost not bite so nigh As be - ne - fits for-

poco rit.

poco rit.

is .... most jol - ly, most

jol - - - - - - ly.

molto vigoroso.

R Q. 1905

BLOW HIGH, BLOW LOW

Charles Dibdin

sig - nal be, to__ think on thee, shall my sig - nal be, to__

rit. *ff a tempo*

think on thee, And this shall be__ my song: Blow high, blow low, let

a tempo

rit. *ff*

tem - pests tear The main-mast by the board; My heart with thoughts of

mp

thee, my dear, And love well stor'd, Shall brave all dan - ger,

mp

flow - ing cans of flip re-new, And drink their sweet-hearts and their wives,

I'll heave a sigh, I'll heave a sigh, and think on thee, And as_ the

ships rolls thro' the sea, The bur-den of my song shall

be: Blow high, blow low, let tem - pests tear The main-mast by the

board;   My heart with thoughts of   thee, my dear,   And love well

stor'd,   Shall brave all   dan-ger, scorn all   fear, The roar-ing winds, the

rag-ing sea, In   hopes on shore   to   be once more   Safe__ moor'd with

thee.

CREATE IN ME A CLEAN HEART, O GOD

Psalm 51: 10-13

Carl F. Mueller

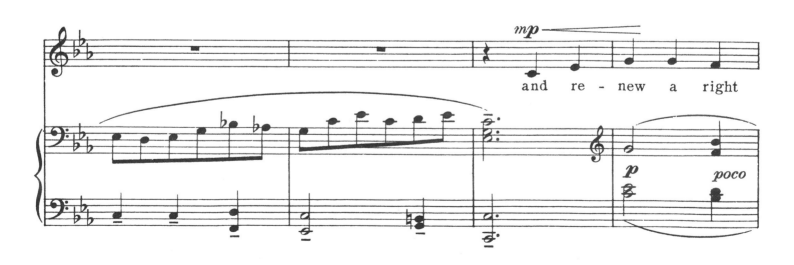

spir-it with - in_____ me.

Cast me not a - way from Thy pres -

ence; and take not Thy ho - ly spir - it from_____ me.

me with Thy free_____ spir-it, Thy free_____ spir - it.

Then will I teach trans-gres-sors Thy ways; and sin-ners shall be con-

vert-ed un-to Thee. Cre-ate in me a clean heart, O God!

"Overlook Acre"
Little Silver, N.J.
July, 1956

ENCANTADORA MARIA
(Maria, Dear)

Latin American folksong
arranged by Edward Kilenyi

En - can-ta-do - ra Ma - ri - a,   Yo te
Ma - ri - a dear, my   pas-sion   and

a-mo con i - lu - sión,_____   A quien le da-ré las que-jas   ne-
great des-pair thou   art,_____   To whom shall I tell the   sor-rows of

-gras de mi co-ra - zón?_____   Ay!_____
my   de - vo-ted   heart?_____   Ay!

FALSE PHILLIS

old English melody, arr. Wilson

meet my_ fair_ Phil - lis,_ and_ tell tales of love,_____

__ But judge of my an - guish, my rage and des-

- pair,_ When I found on ar - ri - val no Phil - lis was

there. I

wait - ed __ a - while, which in - creased but my rage, With __

lov - ers __ you __ know ev - 'ry __ mo - ment's an age, __

I sighed and I cried, and I

looked far and near, __ But in vain was my look - ing, no

Phil - lis was there!

To wait an - y___ long - er I

thought was in vain, So I trudged o'er___ the___ fields to___ my___

cot - tage a - gain;_____ When

Oh! to my grief, in a grove that was near, _____ I be-

-held the false Phil - lis with Da - mon was there.

glowed with_ re - sent - ment, and proud - ly passed by, When,_

THE FRIAR OF ORDERS GREY

William Shield
(1748-1829)

Con spirito

1. I am a Fri-ar of
2. Af-ter supper, of

Or - ders gray, And down in the val - ley I take my way, I
heav'n I dream, But that is fat pul - lets and clout - ed cream; My -

pull not black-ber - ry, haw, nor hip, Good store of venison does
self by de - ni - al I mor - ti - fy, With a dain - ty bit _ of

fill my scrip; My long bead roll I mer-ri-ly chant, Where-ev-er I walk no
war - den pye; I'm cloth'd in sack-cloth for _ my sin, With old _ sack-wine I'm

mon-ey I want, Where - ev - er I walk, no mon-ey I want.
lined_with - in, With old_ sack-wine I'm lined_with - in.

And why I'm so plump, the reason I'll tell: Who leads a good life is
A chirp - ing cup is my mat - in song, And the Ves - per bell is my

sure to live well, Who leads a good life is sure to live well._ 1-2 What
bowl,_ ding, dong, And the Ves - per bell is my bowl, ding, dong._

Bar - on, or Squire, or Knight of the Shire, lives half so well as a Ho - ly Friar, Lives

half so well, half so well, Lives half so well as a Ho-ly Friar? ————

———— As a Ho — — — — — — ly Friar, a

Ho — — — — — ly Friar Lives half so well as a

Ho — ly Friar.

THE KING OF LOVE MY SHEPHERD IS

Charles Gounod

Moderato quasi Allegretto

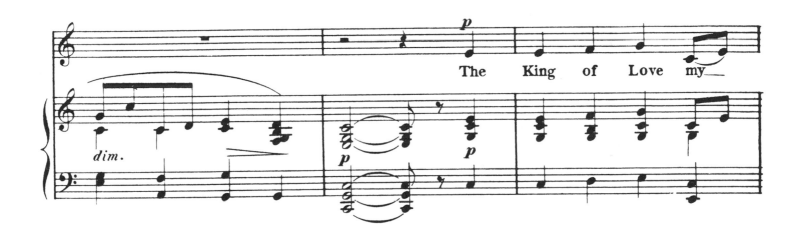

The King of Love my

Shep-herd is, Whose good-ness fail-eth nev-er; I

noth - ing lack if I am His, And He is mine for ev - - er. Where streams of liv - ing wa - ters flow, My ran - somed soul He lead - eth, And where the ver - dant pas - tures grow, With food ce - les - tial feed - - eth.

The King of Love my Shep-herd is,

Per - verse and fool - ish oft I stray'd, But

yet in love He sought me, And on His shoul - der

gent - ly laid, And home re-joic - ing brought me. In

HÖR' ICH DAS LIEDCHEN KLINGEN
(E'er When I Hear Them Singing)

Langsam.
Lento.

Robert Schumann

Hör' ich das Lied-chen klin-gen, das
E'er when I hear them sing-ing The

einst die Lieb-ste sang, so will mir die Brust zer-
song my sweet-heart sang, Wild long-ing a-ris-es,

sprin-gen von wil-dem Schmer-zens-drang. Es
wring-ing My breast with woe-ful pang. Then

treibt mich ein dunk - les Seh - nen hin - auf zur Wal - des -
drives me a name - less yearn - ing To yon - der wood on

hoh', ___ dort löst sich auf ___ in Thrä - nen mein
high; ___ There melts my an - guish burn - ing While

ü - ber-gro - sses Weh.
tears o'er-flow mine eye.

ritard.

INTERMEZZO
(Thine Pure Image)

Robert Schumann

Langsam
Lento

Dein Bild - niss wun - der - se - lig
Thine im - age pure and smil - ing,

hab' ich im Her - zens - grund, das sieht so frisch und
Still in my heart shall stay, With cheer - ful look be -

fröh - lich mich an zu je - der Stund'. Mein
guil - ing Each pen-sire hour a - way. My

poco a poco ac - - - - ce - - - - le -
nach und nach - - - - - - - - schneller - - - - ~

Herz still in sich sin - get ein al - tes, schö - nes
heart se - cret-ly sing - eth An old, me - lo - dious

JAGDLIED
(Hunting Song)

Felix Mendelssohn

Und sind es nicht drei Vö - ge - lein, so
Ich ste - he auf der Lau - er, ich
And if there be no birds there-in, Three
I'll wait a - lone and list - - 'ning Till

sind's drei Fräu - lein fein, soll mir die Ein' nicht wer - -
harr' auf dunk - le Nacht, es hat der A - bend-schau - -
pret - ty maids they be, And will the one not have____
night shall lend her shade; Has twi - light's dew - y glist - -

- den, so gilt's das Le - ben mein,____
- er ihr Herz wohl weich ge - macht,____
__ me, Then life were naught for me,____
- 'ning One heart more ten - der made?____

so gilt's das Le - - - ben mein.
ihr Herz wohl weich _____ ge - - macht.
then life were naught_____ for me.
one heart more ten - - - der made?

3. In's Ju - bel - horn ich
3. My bu - gle sounds a

sto - - - sse, das Fir - ma - ment wird klar,
par - - - ley, The sky is grow - ing bright:

ich stei - ge von dem Ros - - - se, und zähl' die Vö - gel -
To count you all these bird - - - ies I real - ly must a -

schaar. Die Ein' ist schwarzbraun' An - ne, die
light! Why, here is dark - brow'd Nan - cy, And

And - re Bär - be - lein, die Dritt' hat kei - nen Na - - men,
Ka - tie, un - be - known: The third one shall be name - - less,

die soll mein ei - gen sein,_____ mein ei - gen
And she'll be all my own,_____ be all my

sein,_____ die soll mein ei - - -gen
own,_____ and she'll be all_____ my

sein.
own!

THE JOLLY ROGER

Dorothy Foster Brown

R. Ritchie Robertson

*Following the glint of gold to Hell and back again, For they're following the Jolly Roger. Rough, tough sailor-men, naked to the waist, Black and tan and yellow men, lean and evil-faced,

*Optional version: Chasing after plunder to the poles and back again.

Sal - va - dor to Spain, Fol - low - ing the glint of gold to

Hell and back a - gain, For they're following _____ the Jol - ly

Rog - er. Swag-ger-ing ad-ven-tur-ers, with his-to-ries to hide,

Jail-birds and water-rats, cruel, shif-ty-eyed; Out-laws of the Sev-en Seas

poco rit. *a tempo*

fight-ing side by side, For they're following ____ the Jol-ly Rog - er.

poco rit. *a tempo*

Sing a song of pi-rates sail-ing up and down; Some of them will die by steel,

some of them will drown, Some will grace a gallows-tree in a har-bor town, For they're

following _____ the Jol - ly Rog - er. Yo - ho! Yo-

ho! Yo - ho! _____

LA PALOMA BLANCA
(The White Dove)

Latin American folksong
arranged by Edward Kilenyi

LE SECRET
(The Secret)

Armand Silvestre

Gabriel Fauré

Je veux que le ma - tin l'i - gno - re Le
I wish the light of dawn would ban - ish The

nom que j'ai dit à la nuit, Et qu'au vent de l'au - be, sans
name that I told to the night, And on si - lent breeze give it

bruit, Com - me u - ne lar - me il s'é - va - po - re.
flight, That, like a tear, it soon might van - ish.

LEAVE ME, LOATHSOME LIGHT!
from *Semele*

George Frideric Handel

LET US BREAK BREAD TOGETHER

African American spiritual
arranged by Gordon Myers

drink wine to-geth-er on our knees;_____ let us drink wine to-

geth-er on our knees._____ When I fall down on my knees, With my

face to the ris-ing sun, O__ Lord, have mer-cy on me._____

_____ Let us praise God to-geth-er on our knees;_____

Let us praise God to-geth-er on our knees.____

____ When I fall down on my knees, With my face to the ris - ing

sun, O____ Lord, have mer-cy on me, if you

please. Let us break bread to-geth-er on____ our knees.

O MISTRESS MINE

William Shakespeare

Roger Quilter

LORD, I WANT TO BE A CHRISTIAN

African American spiritual
arranged by John Payne

LUNGI DAL CARO BENE
(Far From My Love I Languish)

Giuseppe Sarti

Andante quasi larghetto (♩ = 63)

Lun - gi_ dal ca - ro be - ne,   Vi - ve - re non pos-
Far from my Love I lan - guish,   I do not live, nor

NEXT, WINTER COMES SLOWLY
from *The Faery Queen*

Henry Purcell

ON THE ROAD TO MANDALAY

Rudyard Kipling

Oley Speaks

1. By the old Moul-mein Pa - go - da, look-in'
east - ward to the sea, There's a Bur - ma girl a -
set - tin', an' I know she thinks o' me; For the wind is in the

2. 'Er pet - ti - coat was yal-ler, an' 'er
lit - tle cap was green, An' 'er name was Su - pi -
yaw - lat jes' the same as Thee-baw's Queen, An' I seed her first a -

Copyright renewal assigned, 1935, to G. Schirmer, Inc.

Poco meno mosso

3. Ship me some - wheres east of Su - ez where the best is — like the worst, Where there aren't no Ten Com - mand - ments, an' a man can raise a thirst; For the tem - ple - bells are call - in', an' it's

there that I would be— By the old Moul-mein Pa-
-go-da, look-in' la-zy at the sea, look-in'
la-zy at the sea; Come you back to Man-da-
lay, Where the old Flo-til-la lay: Can't you

THE ROVIN' GAMBLER

words adapted from a folksong

John Jacob Niles

Reelfoot Lake, the background for several of these "Gambling Songs", lies mostly in Tennessee (its northern tip being in Kentucky) and is one of the world's best fishing grounds. Formed by an earthquake in 1811, the lake is surrounded by country abounding in characters who seem to have walked out of the pages of folklore. According to local legend the earthquake was caused by the steamboat "New Orleans" when it made the first steam-powered journey down the nearby Mississippi River.

THE SEA

William Dean Howells

Edward MacDowell

Broadly, with rhythmic swing

One sails a-way to sea, to sea, One stands on the shore and

cries; The ship goes down the world, and the light On the sul-len

wa-ter dies. The whis-per-ing shell is mute, And

af-ter is e-vil cheer; She shall stand on the shore and cry in vain,

SEA MOODS

Kenneth G. Benham*

Mildred Lund Tyson

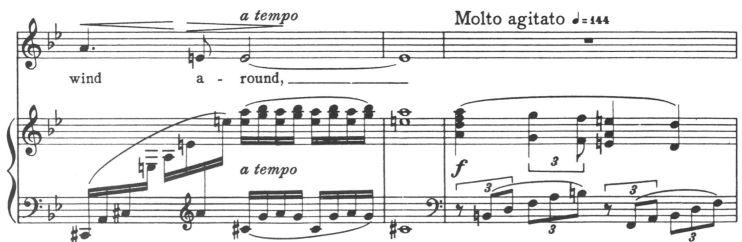

*Words used by special permission.

102

Help me to be _____ Like

you, tri - um - - - phant,

tri - um - phant still! _____

SHENANDOAH

sea chanty
arranged by Celius Dougherty

'Cross the wide Mis - sou - ri.   Mis -

sou - ri she's— a might - y riv-er,   Hi - o! you roll - ing

riv-er,   When she rolls down— her top-sails shiv-er,   Hi -

Shen - an - do - ah,__ I'll not de - ceive you, Hi - o! I'm bound a -

way,

'Cross the wide Mis - sou -

ri._____

THE SPLENDOUR FALLS

Alfred Tennyson

Richard H. Walthew

TALLY-HO!

C. P. Raydon

Franco Leoni

See, here they come with a "View hal - loo!" Hounds and hors-es and hunts - men too,

Gal - lop - ing, gal - lop - ing, gal - lop - ing, gal - lop - ing, gal - lop - ing,

gal - lop - ing, gal - lop - ing by. _____

f

The hors - es tram - ple, the hounds they bay, _____

The rid - ers' coats are scar - let and gay;

cresc.

"Ho there, young - ster!" the hunts - men

cry, "Say, have you seen the fox go by?" Gal - lop - ing, gal - lop - ing, gal - lop - ing,

gal - lop - ing, gal - lop - ing, gal - lop - ing, gal - lop - ing by.

THERE WAS A MIGHTY MONARCH

Ludwig van Beethoven

be. Then calls he for his tail - or: To Court the tail - or

goes: "Here, take the fel - low's meas - ure, And make him brand new clothes!"

In rust - ling silk and vel - vet The flea was gai - ly dress'd He had rib - bons on his should - er; A cross up - on his breast. A min - is - ter they made him, And gave him a star to__ wear; And all his bro - thers and sist - ers Held Court ap - point - ments

there.

court - iers and the lad - ies, A sor - ry time they

The

had! The queen was dread-ful-ly bit-ten; The

maids went nearly mad. And yet they dared not

kill them, Nor make the slight-est fuss. But we will prompt-ly

crack them If they e'er should light on us! But

WHY SO PALE AND WAN?

Sir John Suckling

Thomas Arne

WIDMUNG
(Dedication)

Wolfgang Mueller

Robert Franz